FROM THE DESKTOP OF JEFFREY SIMMONS

A vacation in Paris inspired Miroslav Sasek to create childrens travel guides to the big cities of the world. He brought me *This is Paris* in 1958 when I was publishing in London, and we soon followed up with *This is London*. Both books were enormously successful, and his simple vision grew to include more than a dozen books. Their amusing verse, coupled with bright and charming illustrations, made for a series unlike any other, and garnered Sasek (as we always called him) the international and popular acclaim he deserved.

I was thrilled to learn that *This is New York* will once again find its rightful place on bookshelves, and I would like to thank Judith Stonehill and Barbara Cohen of New York Bound Books for their help and enthusiasm in bringing this wonderful gem to the attention of Universe Publishing. Sasek is no longer with us (and I have lost all contact with his family), but I am sure he would be delighted to know that a whole new generation of wide-eyed readers is being introduced to his whimsical, imaginative, and enchanting world.

YOUR NAME HERE

Published by arrangement with Simon & Schuster Children's Books,
a division of Simon & Schuster

This edition first published in 2003 by
UNIVERSE PUBLISHING
A Division of Rizzoli International Publications, Inc.
300 Park Avenue South
New York, NY 10010
www.rizzoliusa.com

*See updated New York City facts at end of book

2007 / 20 19 18 17 16 15 14 13 12

Printed in China

ISBN-13: 978-0-7893-0884-9

Library of Congress Catalog Control Number: 2002115836

Cover design: Paul Kepple @ Headcase Design
Universe editor: Jane Ginsberg

M · SASEK

THIS IS NEW YORK

UNIVERSE

Amsterdam, November 5, 1626.

High Mighty Sirs:
Here arrived yesterday the ship
The Arms of Amsterdam, which
sailed from New Netherland
out of the Mauritius River
on September 23; they report that
our people there are of good
courage and live peaceably,
they have bought
the island Manhattes from
the wild men for the value
of sixty guilders.
The cargo of the aforesaid
ship is:
7246 beaver skins,
175 ½ otter skins,
48

"Okay, okay, I'll throw in another clock."

In the year 1626 a Dutchman, Peter Minuit, bought the island of Manhattan from the Native Americans for twenty-fours dollars worth of handy housewares. It remains the biggest bargain in American history. Businessmen say that now he would have to throw in another eight billion dollars.

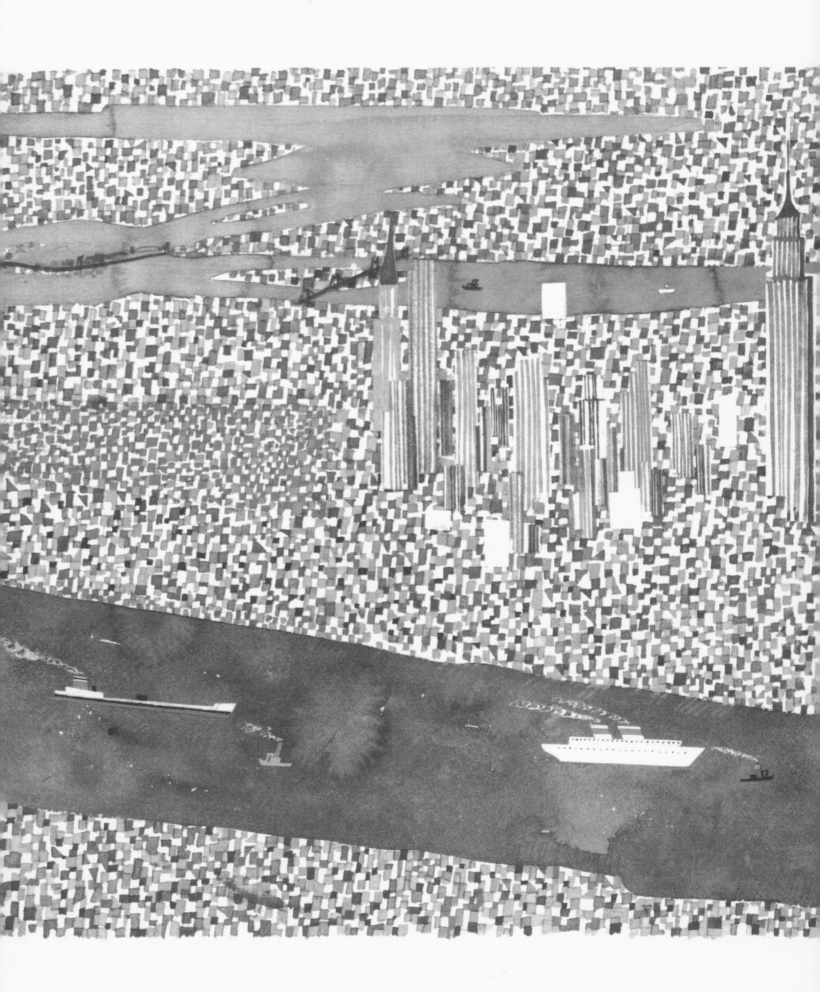

And no wonder.

New York is the largest city in the Western Hemisphere,
and it is full of the Biggest Things.

One of the tallest buildings
in the world —
the Empire State Building.*

1,472 feet high,
102 floors,
74 passenger elevators,
and the most spectacular
views from the top.

The biggest cars

Times Square

— and the biggest traffic jams in the world.

The biggest stretch of streets
to be policed — 6,000 miles
of them.

The biggest Sunday papers.

One of the biggest ports in the world.* Thousands of vessels yearly call at its piers.

The Statue of Liberty,
the largest lady in the world from whose
head (10 feet wide from ear to ear) you can
watch the city skyline and the busy sea.

The biggest ships dock along the Hudson in midtown Manhattan.

New York City consists of five boroughs
— Manhattan, Brooklyn, Queens, The
Bronx, and Richmond (Staten Island).

Here is the Staten Island ferry.

The greatest humidity and heat attack New York in
summer, New Yorkers counterattack with air-conditioners.

The biggest meat-eater of all times — Tyrannosaurus —
can be seen in the New York Museum of Natural History.

When all the air-conditioners
are turned on at one time,
cables burn out and
"dig we must."

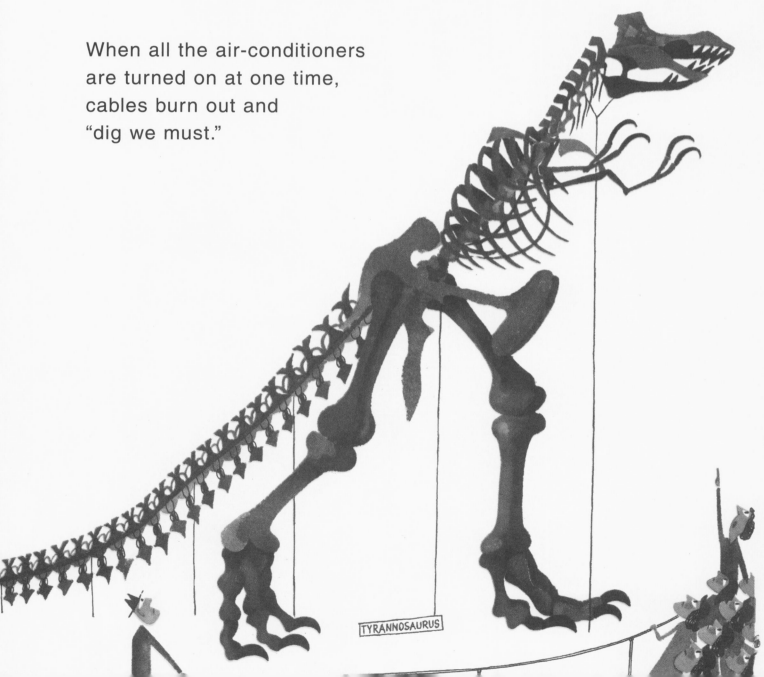

TYRANNOSAURUS

The biggest store in the world

— and one of the smallest.

For there are also small things
in this big, big city —

City Hall

There is also a village — Greenwich Village —

with its small streets like Macdougal Alley

— and its small shops.

Trinity Church, the oldest in New York, is not so small as it looks.
Its tower is 280 feet high.

There are 4,000 churches, synagogues, mosques,
and temples in the city.

There are organizations to care for the
welfare of your body

— of your soul

— and of your country.

New York is the home of the United Nations with its more than eighty member countries.* People from all of them are at home in New York.

So you can shop in any language —

in German

Yiddish

Spanish

Czech and Slovak

Hungarian

Italian

Russian

— and even in English!

A supermarket

Can you read this?

歡迎光臨華埠

Its says: FUN YING QUONG LUM WAH FEW.

In other words:

Welcome to Chinatown!

Harlem is uptown.

The police close many streets in New York
so that children can play there.

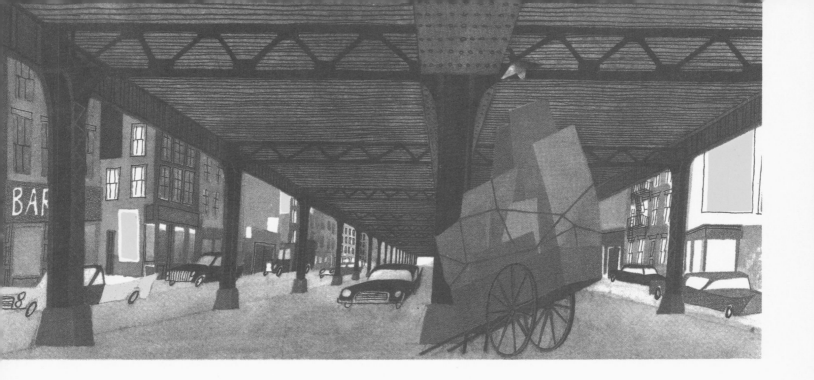

Park Avenue is one of the most elegant avenues of New York.
In Harlem it looks like this.

And here it is, seventy blocks downtown.

This is the elegant way to keep the buildings clean.

All traffic in New York moves up and down.

Down?   Up!

There are 24,000 elevators in the city.*

All the way up on the roofs are water-tanks

— all the way down under ground are the subways. They go in two directions: uptown and downtown.

People walk uptown or downtown

— dresses travel uptown or downtown

— and buses too.

Paying your fare in the bus is like putting
your pennies in a piggy bank.

New York has many tunnels.

This one takes trains into a building

— and this one — the Lincoln Tunnel —
takes cars under the Hudson River.

When you come out you are in the State of New Jersey. From here you see that over on Manhattan almost every building is a skyscraper. Those that are not — will be.

New Yorkers adore to watch them grow.

This one has grown beautifully.

It is the GE Building,
part of Rockefeller Center.
For fun, you can see the
sights from the top or
go skating at the bottom.

You can also skate in Central Park —
even in warm weather

— or feed New York's huge, fluffy squirrels.
They love peanuts.

Peanuts — and
almost everything
else — you can buy
from a machine

— even a pen.

This is Columbus Circle.

"Mail early in the day — it's the better way!"

The George Washington Bridge spans the Hudson.

Brooklyn Bridge, crossing the East River, is the oldest and is popular with everyone from cameramen to songwriters.

From the Brooklyn side, this is Manhattan at night.

In New York fire strikes frequently

— and so do people.

Many fires —
many hydrants
(90,000 of them)*

— and many fire-escapes.

Every six minutes a fire alarm in the city brings out
the engines, motors roaring, bells clanging,
red lights flashing, sirens screaming.*

Hydrants can also have other uses

— for instance, as little Tony's
starting point in business.

With luck it grows to this:

Big Tony   & Co.

With more luck Tony ends up here in Wall Street.

Its name comes from the wall built here by the Dutch against the Native Americans.

Art—seekers can seek art in more than
two hundred art galleries and nine art museums
in New York City.* This one is built by
Frank Lloyd Wright.

On the beach of Coney Island one million sun—seekers
seek sun on a summer Sunday.

Yankee Stadium

Baseball or football fans — 70,000 strong —
come here to watch their heroes.*

Everything in America comes
wonderfully wrapped

— including football players.

A drugstore

You can get everything here from bath soap to bicycles,
from hamburgers to Hamlet.

And here is Times Square, the "biggest supermarket" of them all — frankfurters, hamburgers, aromarama, burgerama, movies, people, cars, lights from dawn to dawn.

A few steps uptown on Broadway,
watch for the weather star high above.

When it is orange, look out!
But when it is green, get ready
for another lovely day in New York!

THIS IS NEW YORK . . . TODAY!

*Page 10: In 1960 the tallest building in the world was the
Empire State Building. Today it is the
Twin Petronas Towers in Malaysia.

*Page 14: In 1960 the biggest port in the world was in New
York. Today it is in Singapore.

*Page 23: Today the United Nations has more than 190
member-nations.

*Page 32: Today there are 67,000 elevators in the city.

*Page 49: Today there are 110,000 fire hydrants in the city.

*Page 50: Today a fire alarm sounds every 30 seconds
in the city.

*Page 55: Today there are more than 450 art galleries and
more than 100 museums in the city.

*Page 56: Today only baseball is played at Yankee Stadium;
the Giants played their last game there in 1973.